Name.. Date..................................

Write over the dotted letters and colour the picture.

I am Tigga.

I am Tigga.

I am Tigga.

Write **I am Tigga** on the dotted line by yourself.

Book 1 Activity 1   Handwriting activities from

Name.. Date..

Write over the dotted letters and colour the picture.

I am Fluff.

I am Fluff.

I am Fluff.

Write **I am Fluff** on the dotted line by yourself.

....

Book 1 Activity 2

Handwriting activities from Jellly and Bean

Name.. Date..

Write over the dotted letters. Then write the sentence by yourself.

I am on the bed.

....

Book 1 Activity 3 Handwriting activities from Jellly and Bean

Name.. Date..

Draw a line from each word to the correct place on a picture.

Write Tigga, Fluff and Bella on the line below..

....

Book 1 Activity 4

Handwriting activities from Jellly and Bean

Name.. Date..

Draw a line from each sentence to the correct place on the pictures.

Tigga can run.

Fluff is in.

Fluff can run.

Tigga is out.

The cat flap is shut.

Book 1 Activity 5   Handwriting activities from Jellly and Bean

Name.. Date..

Draw a line from each word to the correct picture.

| stuck | sack | sock | duck | ck |

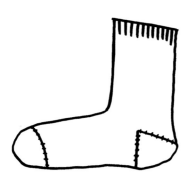

Write each word by yourself. ....

....

Book 1 Activity 6

Handwriting activities from Jelly and Bean

Name.. Date..

Write over the dotted letters and words. Write the words 'jam' and 'bun' by yourself.

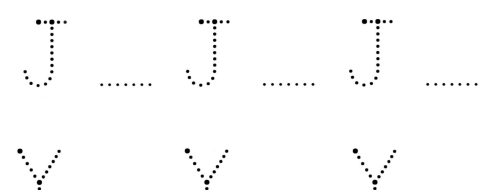

j j j j j j

y y y y y y

Write a small 'j' and y' next to the capital letters.

J .... J .... J ....

jam ....

bun ....

Y ..... Y ..... Y .....

Book 2 Activity 1

Handwriting activities from Jellly and Bean

Name.. Date..

Write the correct word under each picture.

| lick | mess | rub |

....

Name.. Date...

Draw a line from each word to the correct place on the picture.

bun

jam

pop

sink

tap

Tom

Write the missing letter in each word below.

j__m bu__ __om sin__

Book 2 Activity 3

Handwriting activities from Jellly and Bean

Name.. Date..

Draw a line from each word to the correct place on the picture.

top

Tom

peg

sun

Write the missing letter in each word below.

Book 2 Activity 4

Handwriting activities from Jelly and Bean

Name……………………………………… Date………………………………………

Draw a line from each sentence and each phrase to the correct picture. Colour the pictures.

a jam bun

a mess

red jam

I can rub.

I can lick.

The jam drips.

Book 2 Activity 5

Handwriting activities from Jellly and Bean

Name... Date...

Write the correct word in each sentence.

| jam | is | drips |

Tom rubs the ……… .

The top ……. pink.

The top …………… .

Book 2 Activity 6

Handwriting activities from Jelly and Bean

Name.. Date..

Follow the lines and write the correct word at the end of each.

| Tom | box | bus | truck |

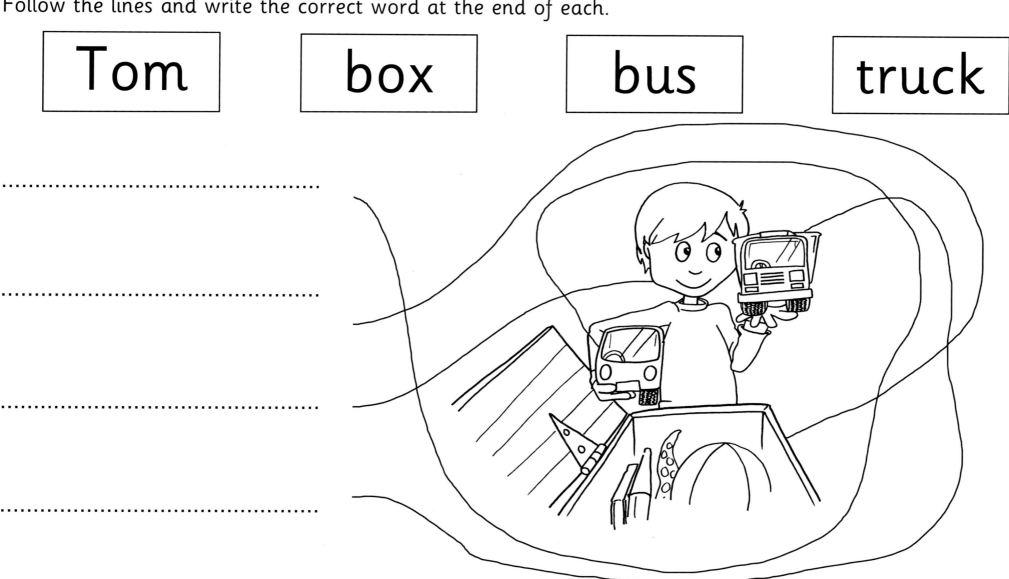

Book 3 Activity 1

Handwriting activities from Jellly and Bean

Name.. Date..

Draw a line from each phrase to the correct picture.

| go fast | press press | on the path |

Write **go fast** on the dotted line.

....

Book 3 Activity 2 — Handwriting activities from Jelly and Bean

Name.. Date..

Draw a line from each word to the correct place on the picture.

Bella   bus   doll   truck

grass   path

Book 3 Activity 3

Handwriting activities from Jellly and Bean

Name.. Date..

Which phrase matches each picture. Write the correct phrase below each picture.

| in the box | set off | bump bang |

 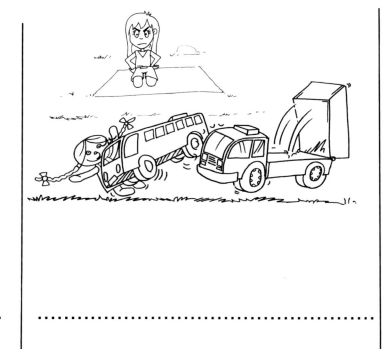 

....

....

Book 3 Activity 4　　　　　　　　　　　　　　　　　　　　Handwriting activities from Jelly and Bean

Name.. Date..

Write the correct word in each sentence.

| mad | is |

| doll |

Bella is ....

Tom .... sorry.

The bus is on top of the ....

Book 3 Activity 5

Handwriting activities from Jellly and Bean

Name.. Date..

Write the correct words in the sentence.

| bus | | box |

truck

Tom puts the ....

and the .... back

in the ....

Name.. Date..

Write over the dotted letters. Join each picture to the correct sentence.

I am Dot.

d D d D d D

d D d D d D

I am Dash.

Book 4 Activity 1

Handwriting activities from Jelly and Bean

Name.. Date..

Write the correct words in the sentences.

| big | little |
| see | bee |

Dot is a .... dog.

Dash is a .... dog.

Dash can .... a .... on Dot.

Book 4 Activity 2

Handwriting activities from Jelly and Bean

Name.. Date..

Draw a line from each phrase to the correct picture.

Run, Dot, run.

Jump, Dash, jump.

Go, Dash, go.

Book 4 Activity 3

Handwriting activities from Jelly and Bean

Name.. Date..

Join the pictures to the correct words. Write each word under the picture.

| jump | hump | bump | lump |

....

....

....

....

Book 4 Activity 4

Handwriting activities from Jelly and Bean

Name.. Date..

Join the pictures to the correct words. Write the missing letter in each word.

si_g   _ang   l_ng   din__

Book 4 Activity 5

Handwriting activities from Jellly and Bean

Name.. Date..

Draw a line from the words to the correct place on the picture. Write the missing letter in each word.

big dog

grass

little dog

bee

_ig   d_g   _ittle   b_e

Book 4 Activity 6

Handwriting activities from Jellly and Bean

Name.. Date..

Draw a line from the words to the correct place on the picture.

| flag | Tom's ship | box |

| brush | | plank |

| grass | | path |

Book 5 Activity 1   Handwriting activities from Jelly and Bean

Name.. Date..

Draw a line from each word to the correct picture.

| ship | Dash | fish | shell | sh |

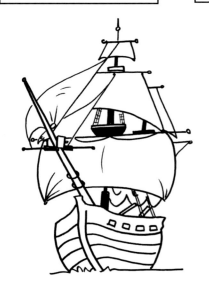   

Write the words ship shell fish Dash on the line below.

....

Book 5 Activity 2 — Handwriting activities from Jelly and Bean

Name.. Date..

Write the correct words in each sentence.

| cup | | hops |

| sits | | parrot |

Tom ....

Bella .... and skips.

Bella has a .... and a ....

Book 5 Activity 3

Handwriting activities from Jellly and Bean

Name.. Date..

Write the correct word in each sentence.

| off |
| drops |
| tips |

Tom jumps ....

The plank .... up.

Bella .... the cup and the parrot.

Name.. Date......................................

Write the correct word in each sentence.

| cross |
| sorry |
| mess |

Tom is ....

Bella is ....

The ship is a ....

Book 5 Activity 5

Handwriting activities from Jellly and Bean

Name.. Date......................................

Which item is missing from the picture?

Write your answer here ....

plank

brush

Bella

parrot

cup

box

peg

Tom

flag

Book 5 Activity 6

Handwriting activities from Jellly and Bean

Name.. Date....................................

Write a line from each word to the correct place on the picture. Write the words on the dotted lines.

Tom

bucket

hen

hut

basket

Bella

....

....

Book 6 Activity 1 — Handwriting activities from Jelly and Bean

Name.. Date..

Draw a line from each sentence to the correct picture.

| The hens peck the seeds. |

| A hen pecks Bella. |

| A hen pecks Tom. |

Draw a line from each word to the correct place on the pictures.

hat   hen   nest   sit   neck   leg   jump

Name.. Date....................................

Write the correct word in each sentence.

| chin | cheek | seven |

The hen pecks Bella on the ....

The hen has .... chicks.

The hen pecks Tom on the ....

Name.. Date....................................

Write a line from each word to the correct place on the picture.

Tom

eggs

hen

lamp

hut

basket

Bella

nest

How many eggs can you see? ....

Book 6 Activity 4

Handwriting activities from Jellly and Bean

Name.. Date...............

Write the correct words in each sentence.

| basket | picks |
| eggs | puts |

Tom .... up the ....

Bella .... the eggs in the ....

Book 6 Activity 5

Name.. Date..

Write the correct word in each sentence.
Draw a line from each sentence to the correct picture.

| see | feed | seeds |

The hens peck the ....

Tom and Bella go to .... the hens.

Tom and Bella .... the chicks.

Book 6 Activity 6 — Handwriting activities from Jelly and Bean